Whose Baby?

Whose Baby?

Therapy for the Christmas Season in Twelve Parts

Ben Pugh

RESOURCE *Publications* · Eugene, Oregon

WHOSE BABY?
Therapy for the Christmas Season in Twelve Parts

Resource Publications
An Imprint of Wipf and Stock Publishers
199 W. 8th Ave., Suite 3
Eugene, OR 97401

www.wipfandstock.com

ISBN 13: 978-1-4982-0606-8

Manufactured in the U.S.A.

To the people of Eagle's Nest Church

Contents

Preface

THERE IS RATHER A lot that I struggle to like about Christmas. Every year I hope, indeed I pray, that this Christmas will be truly the restful, warm, cosy experience that it is always billed as being.

When I was a bachelor I felt like I simply wasn't part of the party, and I thought this was because I had no kids. I thought that was the reason for my complete and utter horror at the way all the shops fill up with sweaty stressed-out people. I thought the absence of kids in my life was the reason why I found the temporary Christmas-themed shops and tacky Christmas lights so insulting to my eyes. "When you've got kids, then you'll understand," I thought. Christmas is for the children. It's all about seeing their bright eyes when you turn the Christmas tree lights on, and their excited faces when they open their presents.

"Have a great Christmas," people would say on the last day of work as I gathered up my little clutch of cards with their pictures of robins, snowy Victorian streets, jolly bearded men that looked like they'd had one sherry too many, and contrasting wiry depictions of three oriental kings and their camels against a starry night. I would put my cards on the yarn with my fellow bachelors' back at the house. If I had a lot of them and had to move some of John's out of the way, there would be a momentary swell of pride. "Merry Christmas," the cards would all shout back at me. One by one my house mates would pack their bags and be off somewhere for a "family Christmas." I too would normally go somewhere, at least for Christmas Day, perhaps to my brother's. It would not take long before I would realize that I was not having a merry Christmas, just a normal one: a welcome break from work but that was all. In every other respect, I was a good deal less happy than normal.

Perhaps the main reason for this was that Christmas was clearly not only a family time but a romantic high point in the year also, comparable in fact to Valentine's Day, which follows so hot on its heels. Having no one special in my life, it was impossible not to feel sad, much as I would not have begrudged lovers their romantic moments by the fire in their matching reindeer sweaters. The happy times tended to be the few small moments of spiritual enrichment. For example, our church was so cutting edge it almost never sang any old hymns—except at Christmas, but the theological and poetic riches of *Joy to the World* and *Hark the Herald* were always a breath of fresh air to me.

Well, now I am happily married with three gorgeous children. Have I found this "merry" and "happy" yuletide gladness? Have I discovered the magic of Christmas? We have two open fires and the occasional robin in the garden and, yes, our kids' faces really do light up like I imagined when Christmas morning arrives. We have even had snow. The conditions are ideal in which to finally slough off my "humbug" spirit and enter into the "spirit of Christmas."

I still find it to be a good break from work, a chance to do lots of completely un-work-related things. In fact, it is the only point in the year when as a nation we (more or less) stop. With "January sales" now beginning the day after Christmas (we call it "Boxing Day" in the UK) and so many shops open as normal all the way up to New Year's Eve, even this welcome full-stop on the life of a nation is being slowly rubbed out. It is no surprise that the melancholic cover version of the Tears for Fears classic *Mad World* was such a big hit a few years back. It is, in so many ways, a mad time of the year. Every night the streets of Nottingham where I live are full of drunk people. Hospital emergency departments fill up with the results of people's stupidity. Everyone seems to have gone berserk. So I still don't feel as though I'm part of that party. But surely now that I have kids in wide eyed wonder, and real log fires (though I try to keep these two things separate if I can), surely now I can see what the true spirit of Christmas is all about.

Well, there are still some barriers for me to overcome. There is, as every parent knows, the constant pressure to spend money you haven't got on things your kids don't need. You try and try to maintain the simplicity of Christmas, and you even talk of doing it differently one year: going away, or serving the homeless, anything just to lift your children out of the crass materialism that is constantly thrown at them from their peers and by advertising. Then, if you have very young children, Christmas, though a break from work, is hardly restful. It's harder work than ever. You go back to work for a break. Then there is the pre-Christmas frenzy. Again, opting out of this is easier said than done. Calendars and diaries and to-do lists are suddenly filled to overflowing. Evening after evening is taken up with one event after another: multiple work dos, spouse work dos, school, church, house group. Every organization you have anything to do with at all seems to want to throw some kind of celebration and either invite you to it or ask you to help out with it in some way. Finally, despite Christmas being the busiest time of the entire year for most churches, the thing we are actually celebrating—even if you are a church-goer—always lies helplessly buried beneath a pile of other stuff. And this is never remedied, despite all the church posters urging us to get back to the Christ of Christmas. It never happens. And I doubt whether Christmas, in its full-blown post-Victorian sense, was ever really about the incarnation of the Son of God. He will always be a subtext, a footnote: By the way, this is the reason we celebrate Christmas. He has never been the true heart of this immoveable feast.

Just what is this illusive thing called a "merry Christmas"? What is the "Christmas spirit"? People of other religions do not celebrate it, of course. People I know who are of another faith seem to dislike it almost as much as I do, yet their non-participation points to this being a specifically Christian feast. Yet—and I know I am hardly the first person to have pointed this out—there is almost nothing Christian about it; almost the reverse is the case. It is a vestige of that curious phenomenon called Christendom, this odd version of Christianity that seemed more like its opposite but which was the dominant religion of Europe for nearly two millennia: the wealthy, powerful, state-sanctioned kind. Christmas is a reminder to us of what that was like. It is a vestige of how the whole of European culture worked: avowedly Christian to the very core yet amassing so many religious trappings and guilty of so much greed and violence that the real Christ was nowhere to be seen. Sure, there was much that was good, but a great deal of it was like the Mad World of the Tears for Fears song: an exercise in missing the point.

Hence, this book. You may well be a lot better at getting into the Christmas spirit than I am and, don't get me wrong, I'm not on some moral crusade here. Probably the main reason why I struggle to like Christmas is that I'm just a miserable so-and-so, and it certainly isn't the case that I have some superior moral or spiritual insight about it. This much I know, though, there are reasons why, at this time of year, we "ought rather to mourn." Before we feast, we need to mourn the centuries of distortion of the Christian faith of which Christmas is a small reminder. This distortion led, not merely to religious silliness: bare-bummed cherubs and other baroque excesses in church architecture (the equivalent to Christmas tinsel perhaps), it led to more sinister things such as the crusades and the inquisitions. A compromised and distorted Christianity can become, not merely frivolous, but positively dangerous.

I'd like to invite you now to pray this with me before we begin:

Prayer: Heavenly Father, I mourn the results of the wrong kind of Christian faith that we see at Christmas time and I ask that, in this culture that has been so affected by it, you would bring your healing and release people from their indifference to Christian faith. And, in my life this Christmas, I invite you to uncover to me again the real Jesus and the wonder of your gift to the earth. Amen.

1

Conceiving the Impossible

IT WAS THE HOUR of the morning sacrifice. It was autumn. The first glow of dawn had given the signal for the three trumpet blasts that announced the opening of the two great gates of the temple courts to let in a steady trickle of worshippers to take part in the daily service. There would be a whole burnt offering of a lamb, followed by the high moment of the service: the offering of incense upon the golden altar in the Holy Place. Zacharias was on duty that day. By lot he was chosen to perform this holy act that could happen only once in any priest's lifetime. The offering of the incense represented the prayers of the nation of Israel. This was an awesome privilege: something to boast of to the grandchildren—except, in Zacharias' case, there were no grandchildren; no children either, since Elizabeth his wife had never been able to get pregnant and was now in her sixties. Zacharias was accompanied by two assistants, also chosen by lot. The first assistant reverently swept away what remained of the previous day's incense offering, bowed and made his exit. The other assistant dutifully poured on fresh live coals taken from the burnt offering, bowed and left. It was now for Zacharias to do his part: spread a handful of incense powder upon the golden altar. A cloud thick and sweet soon spread to the faithful gathered outside. Back inside, as the incense cloud thinned, a figure was discernable to the right of the altar. The bright figure announced that Elizabeth was to conceive and bear a son: John.

Meanwhile, there is Nazareth. Every home was on a hillside, every road a terrace and every view panoramic. The scene at Nazareth was always a busy one full of traders from east and west converging at this place en route to somewhere else. The valley in view from most homes was Jezreel, the location of legendary Armageddon, the scene of countless battles for possession of this little corridor of land, and the famed location for the last battle of all. Mary, engaged but still living with her parents, had been faithfully carrying out the household chores. She was, if anything, slightly more diligent than before out of recognition for all the help that her parents were giving towards her wedding to Joseph, a God-fearing, handsome carpenter. Suddenly, the angel Gabriel appeared in the middle of the dustiest, grubbiest part of the house while Mary wrung out some clothes. He greeted her like she was some great figure of the past, some great saint, telling her she was "highly favored" and that the Lord was with her. It was this greeting that troubled her more than anything. Gabriel explained that she was to bear a son: Jesus. How? She had not had sex with Joseph and would not dream of doing so until her wedding day. The explanation was that "the Holy Spirit will come upon you and the power of the Most High will overshadow you." Because of this work of the Spirit, the son who was to be born would be called the Son of God. Further evidence, he explained, that God was doing this was that he had already brought about an impossible conception in the womb of Elizabeth, her aging relative, for, "with God, nothing shall be impossible."

All of us may have hopes and dreams of a brighter future and a better life but, for the most part, these aspirations are humanly realizable. Of course God is interested in those but there are times when he wants to conceive an ambition, an objective, a great thing within us that is, humanly speaking, impossible. In fact, this always tends to be the kind of thing he impregnates us with: impossible things. This is how God causes us to hope only in him: "For hope that is seen is not hope, for who hopes for what he already sees?

But if we hope for what we do not yet see, we eagerly wait for it with perseverance." (Rom. 8:24–25)

William Wilberforce was a sociable Member of Parliament who enjoyed the glamorous parties and his nice life. An early friendship with the hymn writer John Newton had brought him to faith during his youth but he had drifted from his earlier devotion. He was in favor of the abolitionist cause but not greatly affected by it or by the frequent lobbying from those devoted to the cause. Slowly, he began to recover his faith and became alert to the various social justice issues of the day. One night, he was alone with some statistics about the death rate of slaves in transit from West Africa to the West Indies: 12 percent en route, plus other fatalities before the slaves even boarded, besides many further deaths from various diseases within a year of landing in the West Indies. Altogether, the death rate was about 50 percent. This got to him. The odds of overwhelming vested interests would be stacked against him but an impossible dream was conceived in his heart that day. Later, in a speech, he related how, "from that moment I resolved that I would not rest until I had effected its abolition." Twenty years passed and almost every year he brought the same bill to Parliament. Often, Parliament was distracted by the turmoil in France, or by the health of the king. At its most attentive, general agreement in principle was offered but with a need for more evidence, or sometimes a gradual transition proposed. Finally, on March 25, 1807, a majority vote was cast: slavery would be abolished throughout the British Empire. A touching speech was given in praise of Wilberforce, followed by an act normally not permitted in the House of Commons: applause, and more than applause: a lengthy standing ovation with cheers and roars of support for the man who presently sobbed uncontrollably into his hands. He had conceived the impossible and brought it to birth.

Mary's response to the news from Gabriel has been described as one of "quiet heroism."[1] A betrothal was sacrosanct, especially in conservative Galilee. To be accused of being unfaithful during an engagement was the same as being caught committing adultery

1. Morris, *Luke*, 82.

in a marriage, and such a crime was very serious. Unless she could be vindicated somehow, it was highly likely that Mary would never get her self-respect back. In a gossiping town, she would never recover her reputation, and she could not expect Joseph's reaction to the news, "I'm pregnant" to be a cool one. But she trusted in the Lord, describing herself as a *doulē*, a "slave." Most English translations offer: "maidservant": "Behold, the maidservant of the Lord. Let it be to me according to your word." She submits to God's plan despite the awful perils of the situation she was now in.

And this, likewise, is often a feature of the things that God would conceive within us. They are not only humanly impossible, they might seem fraught with dangers too. The Eden Network, and other similar projects around the world, is about followers of Christ who sense the call towards "downward mobility." They move—sometimes with young families—from a "nice" area to the downtown area. They move to the local "sink estate," where they form relationships with the local people. Added to this are a few hours of voluntary service every week, which they do alongside their job. I heard of one family that did something very like this in crime-ridden Johannesburg. Others have made the same step into the rough parts of Manchester. What about the local school? What about the gangs: won't their own kids be drawn in or be in danger? All these questions and more go through the heads of those contemplating downward mobility. Without the trustful response of Mary: "Behold your slave: let it be to me according to Word," overcoming such anxieties would be impossible. If God would do great things through us then great trust will be needed. We must submit to God's plan.

Mary, however, was human. She could not, for now, contemplate telling Joseph her news. She must first find confirmation that such an outstanding thing as conceiving the Son of God was real and true. And she proved willing to travel nearly 100 miles to find that confirmation. And so it was that a journey on foot that took five days brought her to the threshold of the home of the only other person she knew that was likely to understand: Elizabeth. The confirmation she sought came fully and immediately. Elizabeth even said that her own baby leapt inside her womb as soon as Mary's greeting was heard. Elizabeth was soon in full prophetic voice: "Blessed is she who believed, for there will be a fulfilment of the things spoken to her from the Lord."

I was once part of a church that was so prophetic that sometimes it seemed as if virtually every Sunday some kind soul was making a bee-line for me, putting a reassuring arm around my shoulder and explaining what the Lord had shown them that morning to encourage me. I wrote down everything that was said to me. Their collected sayings eventually filled 13 sides of A4 paper, which I still have. A confirming word can be the difference between a big idea finally coming to birth and it being dismissed in the face of difficulty or long-delayed fulfilment. Imagine what would happen if every church was a church filled with prophetic confirmers each one primed with a word in season to him who is weary.

So, conceive the impossible: get God's dream for your life, submit to God's plan, and seek confirmation. You could do great things for God.

Text: Luke 1:26–45; Matt. 1:18–25.

Prayer: Lord, may the Holy Spirit come upon me and the power of the Most High overshadow me, and may that which He conceives in me find fulfilment according to Your plan, and be for the blessing of the world. Amen.

2

He Has Done Great Things

AND SO IT WAS that Mary, legs aching from five day's walking on uneven dusty roads, could finally sit down. Never had a couch looked so good. Both their faces still shone with gladness: the woman in her sixties marveling at the wonders of God as she looked down into the face of a seated teenager who, by now, was aware within herself that her biology was changing and that she had conceived.

On the way over to Elizabeth's house, Mary had been pondering some of the words of biblical Hannah that she spoke on the day God gave her a son, the legendary Samuel. Hannah famously sang of the great reversal: God lifting up the beggar from the ash heap but sending the rich away empty (1 Sam.2:1–10). These words resonated with Mary as she thought about her own insignificance. Why should God choose her?

Now, the Holy Spirit was filling both Elizabeth and Mary with joyful inspiration. Soon, Mary's words were flowing:

> My soul magnifies the Lord
> And my spirit has rejoiced in God my Savior
> For he has regarded the lowly state of his maidservant
> For behold, henceforth all generations will call me blessed

For he who is mighty has done great things for me
And holy is his name . . .

Let's focus on two phrases here. Firstly, ". . . he has regarded . . ." We have lost touch with him now, but my wife and I once knew a remarkable man. He was born in India but moved to Sri Lanka with his parents, and subsequently to England where he had lived for the past forty years. He appeared in the local and national press as well as on national television to tell his story. His life was never the same when the Tsunami hit Sri Lanka. Within days he was called to go to Sri Lanka not knowing what to expect. He found himself having to identify the bodies of nineteen members of his family that had perished in the disaster, including mother, father, brothers, and sisters—there were few survivors. Even a couple of the survivors subsequently died of grief over the loss of their loved ones. This ordeal led to a breakdown and a prolonged stay in Sri Lanka, during part of which he was kept under observation in a hospital owing to his psychological state. On his return to England, he found that his apartment had been taken off him and all his furniture removed. He also found that, due to a misunderstanding, there was, for the time being at least, no job to go back to. My wife, Pearl, met him at this time at a soup kitchen for the homeless. By this time, he had already dowsed himself in petrol only a week or so before. The match was about to be struck when a stranger, who happened to be a Christian, approached him in the nick of time and said, "You don't want to be doing that mate." It seems, however, that the petrol incident was the nadir. Things started to look better not long after that. He identifies the turning point as being the time when he felt that God had stepped into the situation. Just before meeting Pearl, he had found himself playing host one evening to a remarkable heavenly visitor. He was alone in the dour furniture-less apartment that he had been given as temporary accommodation until the mix up over his original apartment was sorted out. In the corner of the room there appeared a light. He described it to us as rather like a big ball of cotton wool. Gradually this ball of light took on the appearance of a light-filled figure standing in the corner of his room with arms that beckoned to him. The face was not visible due to the intensity of the light. Somewhat alarmed by the sight and not knowing whether he was losing his mind, he called a friend to come and see it. She came and saw it and calmly said to him, "I think God's trying to show you He's looking after you." After a few moments had passed, he ventured to touch the angel. When he did so, the figure lifted up its arms and vanished upwards. In the course of time, he got his job back, got his apartment back (although no-one ever did manage to trace the furniture) and he soon began work rebuilding the hotel that his parents had run in Sri Lanka, and re-employed all the original surviving staff. He has married a lady he has known since childhood and has had a house built for the two of them in their beloved Sri Lanka and has now returned there. And his faith? The last time we spoke to him, it was clear that his faith had never been stronger. Whenever we met him, his cheerful heart was full of thanks to God for all He had brought him through. God stepped in. He regarded him.

Nowhere near as heart-rending as losing your family was my experience of my very first term at art college as an eighteen year-old lad. I simply was not making any friends. It's not as if I didn't look the part: long hair, psychedelic clothes, beads, although I have to say, my fellow art students mostly did not look the part. In fact, one of them was a former accountant. I felt desperately lonely. All the while a phrase kept turning over in my mind as I wondered the corridors of the college: "I don't know what I'm doing, where I'm going, or why." One rainy day, I ended up sitting in a bandstand in a park and sobbing. I attempted my first ever prayer (apart from those of the, "please don't let the teacher pick me" kind). I asked God for two friends: one male, the other female. The female friend is another story for another occasion, but the male friend turned out to be the one who would later listen to my disillusionment about my experiences of life and love since leaving the parental nest (classic quarter-life crisis). Hearing me, he said, "Well, you know what the answer is, don't you?" I said, "Jesus." This kicked off two months of talking about Jesus and noticing that whenever we did so, his presence could be felt, and then to more experiments with praying to this presence whenever I was alone in my room. Before long, I had handed my life over to Christ. That was 26 years ago. He regarded my lowly state. He came near, and my life was never the same again. A few years later, having joined a lively charismatic church, there was a song that always made me think back to that bandstand: "Your love surrounded me from the start; I never want to be apart from you ever again."

The next phrase to look at is, "for he who is mighty has done great things for me, and holy is his name." As with all four of the great praise songs of the infancy narratives, Mary here speaks mostly in the prophetic past. The longings of Israel are now so assured of fulfilment that she speaks of them as already done: "He has shown strength with his arm . . . He has scattered the proud . . . He has helped his servant Israel."

When we lived in a village there was a gate that I would visit that looked out across some undulating fields. I came to call it my Grateful Gate. I would visit it on a summer's evening and there remember all of God's kindnesses to me. On the first occasion, I looked back across a mere six years with amazement. These had been years in which I had gone from being single to being happily married with (at that time) two beautiful little girls. I had gone from having only a degree in art to having an MA and a PhD in theology—my very title had changed. I had gone from trying to get by with visiting lecturing and with a part time job in a call center, where every 10 minute break was timed, to having recently been appointed as Director of what was reputed to be one of the largest theological graduate schools in Europe. I had gone from living in a dark, cold bachelor pad in a town that one of my fellow bachelors would describe as the Armpit of Hampshire to a little cottage in Nottinghamshire with a long thin garden leading to open fields at the back where the swallows would swoop and the buzzards would soar. I wanted to pinch myself. "Is this real?" I thought. "Is this really my life, or am I watching someone else's? Or perhaps some romantic film with a sugary happy ending that the screen writer has made up?" He who is mighty had done great things for me, and yet greater things have followed. Sure, life's not always a bed of roses for me any more than for anyone else. Life has its pressures, but he has continued to "show strength with his arm."

Text: Luke 1:39–55

Prayer: Lord, thank you for the ways in which, at times when I have been at my lowest, you have shown that you regarded me (now, pause to bring these times to remembrance and thank him).

And Lord, thank you for the impossibly great things you have done for me, for all the things that were once a longed for dream but which are now an everyday reality (pause once again to name them).

I confidently look to you for yet greater things (name these). Amen.

3

No More Groundhog Days

ZACHARIAS, LOCKED WITHIN A silent world for nine months—and it is believed that the angel in the temple had struck him deaf as well as dumb—pondered long and hard on the last liturgical words he spoke, just prior to the casting of lots that decided which priest would be honored with the once-in-a-lifetime opportunity to offer incense upon the golden altar. They had been the words of the *Eighteen Benedictions,* which open with: "Blessed are you, O lord our God and God of our fathers, God of Abraham, God of Isaac, and God of Jacob, the great mighty and revered God, the most high God, who bestows loving kindness, and the Master of all things; who remembers the pious deeds of the patriarchs, and in love will bring a redeemer to their children's children for your Name's sake . . ."

The day had now come to circumcise the child of Elizabeth's barrenness. After the cutting and the ceremonial cup of wine, more liturgical prayer ensued as part of the naming ceremony: ". . . and let his name be called in Israel Zacharias, the son of Zacharias." Elizabeth needed to stop this freight train of liturgy that was about to set its seal on something that she already knew from Zacharias was not to be. There was no gentle way to do this: "No!" she shouts, "His name will be John!"

An awkward silence begins, interrupted only by the quiet cries of her new-born still smarting from his wound. She is rebuked by the friends and relatives present: "But there is no one among your relatives who is called by that name."

Zacharias was handed a wooden tablet coated with wax. "Yoẖanan shimō," he writes emphatically, "His name is John." There is to be no negotiation. At that moment, the silence that had descended because of unbelief was suddenly turned into the loud and exuberant cries that come from a heart filled with faith. His tongue was loosed and his hearing restored. Now his heart brimmed with the knowledge that all the future tenses of the *Eighteen Benedictions* ought now to be expressed in the past. They were as good as done. Why? Because the great day of the Messiah was now dawning, and his baby son would prepare the way. No longer can he say the words, ". . . and in love will bring a redeemer." Now it has to be: "Blessed is the Lord God of Israel, for he *has* visited and redeemed his people . . ."

Not until half way through his benediction, however, does Zacharias turn to his own boy, look into his tiny face, and allow himself that glow of fatherly pride. Yet, even then, the role assigned to John, though great, is great only in so far as it points to one yet greater. John the Baptist would later be described as the greatest of all the prophets, and "more than a prophet" (Luke 7:26). How immeasurably great then, must the one be of whom the adult John would one day say, "I am not worthy to untie his sandal straps." The ageing Zacharias cradles the infant John and says to him:

> "And you, child, will be called the prophet of the Highest;
> For you will go before the face of the Lord to prepare his ways.
> To give knowledge of salvation to his people by the remission of their sins,
> Through the tender mercy of our God,
> With which the Dayspring from in his has visited us;
> To give light to those who sit in darkness and the shadow of death,
> To guide our feet into the way of peace."

The 1993 film *Groundhog Day* charts the misadventures of a weatherman who finds himself woken up at the same time every day by his alarm clock and is then forced to live exactly the same day as yesterday, over and over again until he knows off by heart exactly what everyone he meets is about to say and do. This was such a great concept it has been pastiched a number of times since. In particular, in *Evan Almighty* of 2007, Steve Carrel plays a congressman who starts finding himself woken up at 6:14am every day by his alarm clock. It turns out that God, via his alarm clock, is trying to draw his attention to Genesis 6:14 and commission him to be a latter day Noah and build an ark of gopher wood. Then there is *Shrek Forever After* of 2010 in which, because of a casually spoken wish, the ogre finds himself stuck in the same day, with only minor variations to the dull domestication that fills it every time. But here, in Zacharias' benediction, we have an announcement of a Christ who is named the Dayspring or the Dawn. He is the dawning of a brand new day.

The poem draws our attention to three specific areas where the dawning of the new Messianic day will bring its newness . . .

Firstly, there are those who are caught in anxiety and fear. The effect of the new dawn will be that they are released to serve God all their days "without fear" or "fearlessly." Author Fay Weldon was once asked what makes women happy. Her reply was "Nothing for more than ten minutes." The reason for this, she explained, was that women are "wired" in such a way as to make it impossible for them to enjoy themselves for more than ten minutes without worrying about something.[1] Some of us get anxious for no other reason than that we aren't anxious about anything, and really should be. Every now and then, I get that carefree feeling, usually when I'm driving to work. And I think, "Wow! I really haven't got a care in the world." And I muse that, according to the teachings of both Jesus and Paul, freedom from worry and anxiety is actually supposed to be normal. Let the Sunrise from on High break your anxiety-filled Groundhog Day.

---

1. *Breakfast* interview, BBC 1, Wednesday 19 Sep 2006.

Secondly, it is a new day for you if you need the tender mercy of God. The Greek word used to describe this tender mercy refers to the bowels. The same word is used when Jesus is described as being "moved with compassion" for the multitude. It comes from the depths. If you are beset with a sense of failure, if that part of your brain that has been put in charge of self-censure refuses to switch off, even for a moment, then this is for you. Charles Finny experienced an infilling of the Holy Spirit that he described as being, at one stage, like being brushed up and down by enormous wings. At another stage, it was like being filled with liquid love. This love was so intense he had to beg God to stop. Yet I'm quite sure that Finny tasted a mere teaspoonful of God's love that day. Christ is moved to the very depths of his being, to the very bowels, with compassion. His heart goes out to you and his mercy can end your conscience-stricken Groundhog Days.

Thirdly, the breaking of the Messianic dawn means guidance where there is confusion and despondency. It is not for nothing that this passage describes people "sitting" in darkness. It describes that waning of motivation that we feel when we have lost our way, lost our vision. We sit down. We can no longer remember the great purpose to which God has called us and life seems like a merry-go-round that we want to get off. But wherever the Light of the World is welcome, he will shed his light, and will guide our feet into the way of peace.

But how? How does this actually work? Lately, I have been meditating on 2 Corinthians 5:17. I spent a whole week mulling over the phrase, "new creation," and then a week on "old things have passed away." It was in the middle of that week that I finally got to a place, as I lay awake one night, where I simply believed it. A newness is quite naturally coming forth out of Christ in me, because Christ is that new life. He is the source of the newness now coursing through me.

Missionary to Central Africa, Norman Grubb, along with his wife Pauline (nee Studd) came into contact with Jessie Penn-Lewis' "cross teaching" while serving in the Congo in the early 1920s. Her teaching centred around our union with Christ in his death and resurrection. Galatians 2:20, which speaks of our crucifixion with Christ, was the key to Norman's breakthrough: but he had to believe it. His wife had entered into a new victory without difficulty but he was left struggling until one hot night while sat out on the veranda he resolved that he would simply believe it, and reckon it to be so. Soon enough he began to see a change but he had to learn not to look within himself and monitor his progress but always to look away to Christ and let him live his life through him: "He in me is the all, the joy, power, wisdom, victory—all. I transfer my attention, my recognition, my affirmation from the human vessel to Him whom it contains."[2]

Text: Luke 1:57–79.

Prayer: King Jesus, Light of the World, Dawn of the new creation, I invite you to break the fetters of anxiety, of guilt and of confusion and powerfully to live your life in me today. Amen.

---

2. Norman Grubb, *Once Caught, No Escape*, 86.

4

The Day of Small Things

Now in their fourth day of constant travelling, Joseph wondered whether he had ever felt this tired: physically and emotionally. Mary's face, though she was atop their plodding donkey, had accumulated white dust. As a concession to Jewish custom, the Romans had allowed everyone to return to their place of birth to be registered for the census, rather than their place of residence. Some concession! They had not long passed the holy city when Mary reported her first regular contractions. Joseph was anxious and tried to hurry both his own feet and the hooves of the donkey towards the ascent, rising to some 2,500 feet above sea level, to Bethlehem. Mary's face was looking more and more creased with pain. For now, all the portentous events and predictions were gone from their mind as the struggle and grind of survival claimed all their strength. This chilly evening, Joseph was a lather of sweat.

Finally they entered Bethlehem's streets, and fresh waves of anxiety filled Joseph's heart at the sight: outside every khan, people were lying and propping themselves up on the walls outside. Beside the road, many were sleeping rough. Every possible place of lodging was occupied. Clearly David's city had birthed a substantial diaspora over the years, which had now returned and meekly rested wherever possible. Mary however, was not so docile. She was leaning forward over the mane of the donkey every five minutes, panting her way through the increasing agony, but trying not to alarm the already stressed out Joseph.

After much pleading a cave was given the couple, the function of which was normally the stabling of livestock. A camel lay there—someone's pride and joy—as well as a sleepy donkey, and a cow. There was much hay, a number of feeding troughs, and a rich dungy sort of smell. Plumes of steam emanated from the exhalations of beasts as the air grew chillier. Joseph made a fire at the entrance and heated some water. Soon enough the more urgent moaning of the final stages of labor began: deep, long groans. Mary was happy for her husband to sit at the entrance and not watch her as she went deeper and deeper into that world of pain that only a woman can know. They had together made a cradle for the baby from the abundance of straw, which they used to line a feeding trough. These were not exactly sterile conditions but the couple was accustomed to making the best of privation.

Joseph sat at the cave's mouth looking out across the vale that stretched out before him dotted with sheep destined for the temple sacrifices. There was an interlude in the panting and long moans of Mary and his eyes began to feel heavy. His head nodded and sleep began to overtake him.

He woke with a start. There was a noise like a baby crying. Could it be? Already? He turned to find Mary grinning and, though pale, she was all aglow with joy. Jesus was taking his first meal of milk.

Black and dominating the skyline this starry night was Herodium, one of Herod's many residences. It was a magnificent fortress. It had baths and pleasure gardens and a small town had grown around its base. That puppet king of the Jews slept well that night in his marble palace beneath his silk sheets. Jesus dozed at the breast while a cow snorted and Mary lovingly plucked a little straw from her baby's head.

In Rome, Caesar Augustus also was sleeping well among the colonnades of his home. Little did he know that in little more than 300 years the empire he ruled would come to reject the veneration of emperors and of the Greek pantheon in deference to "Christianity," a religion based on a man born in a cave.

For now, "Enough for Him," it was, "whom cherubim worship night and day, a breastful of milk, and a mangerful of hay." It was his good pleasure to enter human life in between a stressed and exhausted young couple and in the midst of grime and stench and at a time so inconvenient that there was no space for him in our lives. It is a Christmas sermon cliché to point out the undeniable fact that he has been doing the same ever since.

A young woman once had a dream that she felt had come from God so she shared it at the house group I attended. I remember it because it confirmed an important decision I was in the throes of making at the time. She recounted that in the dream she went for a walk along familiar paths but then noticed a very small opening. She went through it and this new path began to open out into wide and beautiful vistas that she would never have seen had she not taken that one small step through that one easily overlooked opening.

God starts small; so very small we can miss it. A nation started with the elderly Abram, a movement began with a strangely warmed heart, a revival in Ulster once began with a lone weeping boy kneeling in a playground, and the answer to the deepest of human longings was given in a tiny bundle of life in a hay-filled trough.

Noticed any tiny breakthroughs lately? Sensed God beginning to do a small new thing? "Do not despise the day of small things," says the prophet (Zech. 4:10).

5

The Bored Shepherds

THE SCENE WAS A beautiful one and the subject of countless Christmas cards ever since. The sky was full of stars, the air chilly. The sheep lay quietly on the spreading moonlit pasture. Sparks danced from the feeble fire as the shepherds, a despised and isolated profession of men with a reputation for pilfering, huddled in their threadbare blankets. Conversation had dried up now as each passed sleepily into favorite preoccupations or nagging worries, or complete boredom. In fact, the overarching mood was more than likely one of strength-sapping, wonder-less, never-ending, yawn-inducing tedium.

I can remember much of my youth being spent in this state. It was probably part and parcel of being a teenager. The wonderment of childhood had all past and the world seemed to turn grey. I remember cloned supermarket car parks, dull bus rides in the rain, horrible ice-cream van jingles and desperately irritating TV adverts for cut price three-piece suites. All was banal. I longed for another dimension. There had to be more. I developed a fascination with amphibians and kept them in terrariums: exotic ones that I had bought in pet shop. Amphibians, so it turned out, have immense reserves of patience. They can easily sit in the same spot all day long. The most interesting thing to happen was when my leopard frog changed its skin. Normally brightly colored it would start to look dull and sickly, as though about to die. Then, the front paws would begin to vigorously stroke the face. Gradually, something would start to come loose. Folds of skin were visible as he slowly sucked it into the corners of his mouth, gaping periodically. Then, the task complete, he would start to look all perky and bright—and carry on sitting on his favorite rock for the rest of the day.

So, here we are with these bored shepherds. Unexpectedly, a group of sheep begin to rise to their feet. Some let out a bleat. All four shepherds look up from the fire and squint at this sudden movement. Before they can make anything out, a man comes from nowhere and stands right in front of the fire and looks down at each startled man, beaming, grinning from ear to ear. It was clear this was not a shepherd and the men were sufficiently schooled in their tradition to know from the spotless white robe that this was an angel. Terror soon rises within their hearts.

With a command to not be afraid, the angel announced the news. There was born this very night a tiny life that was destined to cast a shadow across all history that would be greater than the greatest, and his salvation would be offered to all people. Then, heaven could no longer contain itself and burst into song: "Glory to God in the highest, and on earth peace to those on whom his favor rests." Open-mouthed the men watched as the angel stood aside to give place to the swarms of angels suspended in mid space moving in formation and singing in exquisite harmony. The night sky was all alight. The most exquisite welling joy cast out the fear from the shepherd's hearts. Slowly, the chorded singing grew quieter, the heavenly light grew dimmer and the angels got smaller until the night sky once again hosted only stars.

Euphoric, almost drunk with cheer, they looked at one another. They had suddenly regained a sense of wonder they had not known since boyhood. All cynicism, bitterness and boredom had fled, giving place to, "Did you see that!?" It was the most amazing thing any of them had ever witnessed.

The angel had given them quite detailed instructions about where they would find this little baby and, once they had calmed down a little, the instructions came back to their minds as they checked the details with each other. Off the four men went into town, not really knowing where to check first. Somehow, God's Spirit was with them and they happened upon a khan where they asked the proprietor if he knew anything. It just so happened that he was the one that had offered his cave to the troubled couple earlier that night. By now, a few of the ladies had found out about the birth and there was some toing and froing of people offering whatever help they could. The shepherds were soon excitedly introduced to the couple with the new baby. The joys of a birth in such an unexpected place had brought delight to a number of other lodgers. The shepherds knelt in reverence before the tiny fragile little boy. This was a homage filled with wonder: a complete and utter marvel precisely because God's greatest intervention in the history of their nation was so tiny and helpless, and yet so beautiful. Tears welled in their eyes. The hopes of a nation were held in the grip of a tiny clenched hand. The mouth that would utter the greatest teachings ever heard began rooting for more milk.

There was much joy that night, and news of the shepherd's angelic encounter travelled fast. Mary stored it all in her heart.

Text: Luke 2:8–20.

Prayer: Lord, would you show me your glory in such a way that my sense of wonder is renewed. Cause my heart to be filled with the awe and gladness of knowing you again, the Desire of All Nations. And this joy let no one take from me. Amen.

6

A Particular People

ALL THREE OF OUR KIDS were born in the dining rooms of two previous homes. These were, and by our own choosing, home water births, and I was the birthing partner. It was my job to keep the water in the birthing pool at 36° for the labor and 37° for the birth. And my job it was also to sex the child and cut the cord, officially and finally severing the new born from life in the womb, and joining him or her to life in our household. Aside from all the feelings too deep to go into here, one of the most dominant impressions left was that of wetness. There was water everywhere. The other impression was that it was messy. Our labors were straightforward compared to the horror stories that the majority of other couples we knew seemed to have. But even straightforward births are messy, difficult, and of course, painful beyond description. My amazing wife is the strongest person I know but even she was taken to the limits of endurance each time. Reuben's birth, in particular—in the dining room of a cramped rented hovel—seemed especially messy and difficult, and I never cease to be amazed at how perfect he turned out to be. And on each occasion, let it be said, we were blessed with the provision of two (and at one stage, three) community midwives who were patient, calm and dedicated.

For Joseph and Mary, just as routines were taking shape in the relative normality that had emerged since that traumatic night full of pain and mess, the time had now come for more pain, more mess. Joseph, with his son now eight days old, needed to perform an operation that he was nervous of doing but which was the duty of the father of a firstborn son to carry out: the circumcision of his son. Joseph and Mary went out to the local synagogue in search of a rabbi who might be able to guide the young Joseph through the process. Circumcisions would normally be a family occasion but this couple was far from home and there were few close relatives living anywhere near.

They sent for a celebrated local teacher and waited at the synagogue for him. It was a chilly morning within these thick stone walls and Joseph was nervous. All was still but the baby was restless, as though he knew the pain that was about to come. Eventually, an aged rabbi shuffled in with all his equipment wrapped in hessian. Though he was old and bent, his eyes were full of life and color. His keen attentiveness to the ways of God had kept his eyes from growing dull. He looked up into Joseph's face and then into Mary's and re-iterated the story of Abraham's circumcision and the circumcision of his son Isaac. This was a solemn sign of the unique covenant that God had made with his people. It was a mark of ownership, evidence that they were his own special people. Now he focused on Joseph and drew nearer to explain what was about to happen. By now, the baby's little cry was beginning to interrupt. The rabbi took the baby and went to the designated place. He began to hand the flint knife to the child's father, repeating his earlier instructions with a gesture through the air before letting Joseph seize the handle. The pain and bleeding involved ensured that there was no possibility of Joseph congratulating himself afterwards with any thoughts of, "that went well." No matter how well he performed the ritual he would feel terrible.

And so he did, but an important step had now been taken. From this moment, Jesus was part of a specific people, a Jew. And this is the marvelous thing. The God of all the earth does not burst in upon his universe. He always starts small and specific. His is a bigness that does big things but always starts with the local and particular. It is a bigness that the Jewish people had been perfectly familiar with from their understanding of the call of Abraham out of paganism to birth a people, and then the call of Moses out of following sheep to rescue them, and then the call of a ruddy, forgotten little lad called David to make them great. That same God was now beginning a new phase in the grand plan. This was the long promised king in the line of David who would extend God's reign into the whole earth. God is big and does big things and is on a big mission, but always starts with someone in particular, some place in particular, at some time in particular. The tiny crying life now being brought out of the synagogue into the bright morning sun was the gleaming but bloodied page of a new chapter in the history of humanity.

Text: Luke 2:21

Prayer: Lord God of the heavens and the earth: you have placed me within a particular people and caused me to be born and grow up at this particular point in history. I long for you to break into your world and triumph over the evils that fill it. Start with my life Lord. Triumph over the evils of my heart and take me on your mission into the world. Amen.

7

Getting Physical

BUNKHOUSE HOLIDAYS, STATIC CARAVANS, camping trips and similar suffering-for-fun type holidays leave me with mixed feelings. They can be really fun, they can be refreshing, they usually bring us back in touch with nature, they are often enormously exciting for children, and they are cheap. Yet there is always something about them that has to be endured. Closer contact with nature inevitably means greater exposure to extremes of cold, wet, wind, snow and (very rarely) heat. Excited children can be hard work: they hurt themselves more often, they seem to get unwell more easily and soon become over-tired and cranky.

They were accustomed to simplicity but Mary and Joseph had been putting up with accommodation that was definitely more in touch with nature and the elements than was normal for them. They had even had their first baby surrounded by livestock. We do not know whether they stayed a whole six weeks in the cave and made the best of it or whether some slightly better accommodation became available but these were not likely to have been forty days of luxury. So it felt good to be loading up the donkey again for the first leg of their journey home. They were setting off on the five miles of undulating roads that would lead them from Bethlehem to the Jerusalem temple. This was for two further ceremonial items that needed checking off: Mary's purification and Jesus' presentation.

The law of Moses dictated that a woman who had given birth would be ceremonially unclean for forty days. An offering of a lamb and a turtle dove was required, but the law, laced as it was with tenderness towards the poor, allowed couples with only the means to buy two pigeons to do so and to offer these instead. Quite what ceremonial impurity was and why it was incurred by such wholly innocent things as menstruation, childbirth, contact with a dead body or the eating of certain kinds of food, is far from easy to answer. That there is a close relationship between what the law of Moses declared was unclean and what we today would class as unhygienic seems very clear, though less so when it comes to the forty days of quarantine that was to follow childbirth. It is also clear, however, that unclean did not equal unholy. It was possible for priests, for instance, to become ceremonially unclean and yet not lose their status as holy priests. Various explanations in Leviticus reveal that the purity laws seem to have had something to do with God being physically present in the midst of Israel when they were in the wilderness, dwelling as a cloud of glory in a tent right at the center of the camp. Hence the purity laws all had to do with physical things. At the time of Joseph and Mary, God's glory was still understood to physically dwell in the Jerusalem temple, demanding a physically (as well as spiritually) worshipful response.

Sometimes I feel that I have most truly connected with God when I have physically got onto my knees, as I did in the conservatory this morning. I often feel deeply moved by acknowledging God's right to be my God in that way. I also feel incredibly safe in that place and, despite the hard floor pressing against my knee caps, I want to stay there. Maybe we could say that the various physical washings and offerings of animals in Jewish rites are something similar: an acknowledgment of God's right to be God over all of life including the physical and the everyday.

Joseph held the baby while Mary went onto the Court of Women. She found herself at the back of a small throng of other women that were there for the same purpose. She went forward and watched while the priest twisted the heads of her pigeons and offered their blood. She then went to kneel before a great cloud of incense and join in with some liturgical prayers. A great joy rose within her heart at the beautiful gift that God had given and she hurried back to Joseph to hold the baby once more.

It was now their solemn duty to find a priest and give their firstborn to him. This was an act of remembrance for the exodus when, at the price of Egypt's firstborn, Israel was delivered. Five Shekels could secure the child's symbolic release from the priest. Alternatively, the child, like Samuel and Samson, could be dedicated to a life of service to God in the temple. We do not know which of these took place. We only know that Luke does not mention the payment of the Five Shekels of redemption money. The baby in the arms of the priest, combined with the historical themes of redemption and deliverance that surrounded the ceremony, caught the attention of an old man called Simeon, whom we will hear from next. For now, let's note this day of physical acts of acknowledgment, of embodied worship and of honoring God, honoring him, that is, with journeying, paying money, bowing, and handing over the most precious thing they had.

Do you get bored and restless sitting there with your eyes closed trying to pray? Does your mind drift? Try getting physical instead.

Text: Luke 2: 22–24

Prayer: Do something physical towards God such as creating a work of art for him, writing a letter or poem to him, traveling to a special place to pray, or bowing or kneeling to him where you are.

8

Now, At Last

THE WORLD QUAKES WHEN there is a "now, at last." Speakers and writers of a variety of ideologies and for a variety of purposes dip into the litany of key dates so much that some of them are almost becoming a cliché. 1807: at last Wilberforce finally succeeds at getting Parliament to approve the abolition of the slave trade. 1989: after decades of prayers and hopes, the Berlin Wall comes down—at last. 1990: at last, Nelson Mandela is freed after twenty-seven years of incarceration during which people sang songs, held pop concerts and celebrated his birthday. 1991: at last apartheid is officially abolished. Anyone in politics and on the right side of the divide at one of these moments must surely think that heaven is smiling on them.

Of my many now-at-lasts probably the one that gave the most joy at the time was the one that came at the end of fifteen years of false starts. I had been on a quest for, not so much a wife necessarily, more anyone at all that might be willing to actually go out with me on an actual proper date and perhaps even become my girlfriend. My own lack of forwardness (admittedly) combined with the endless and complicated prevarications of some girls meant that this was a quest that took me well into my thirties and was quite fruitless. Somehow, nothing seemed to be working out. I discovered the truth of the first part of Proverbs 13:12: "A hope deferred makes the heart sick . . ." The second part: "But when the desire comes it is a tree of life," I could only imagine. I was withering away like a dry old stick.

Following three months of emails and texts, I met my wife face-to-face for the first time one warm June evening in Nottingham having travelled up by train from Aldershot to meet up: a tall, vivacious blond, bubbly enough to help me forget my nerves. We both knew beyond doubt that we were right together and within a couple of weeks we were engaged. The proposal took place at the top of an ancient Roman fortification near Aldershot called Caesar's Camp, from which the lights of London could be seen on a clear night. The sun was setting as we got our breath back after the climb. The nightjars were making their primordial rattling sound from the heath. I said, "The sun is setting on my old life and rising on a new life with you. Will you marry me?" OK, at this point she burst out laughing but ten years and three kids on, here we are, happy as can be.

For so long had Simeon made the short walk to the Temple to look at the baby boys being presented that a constant battle with self-doubt was fought within his mind. A very clear impression had been given him by God that the long promised Messiah was just about to come. Yet, the word 'come,' is probably not enough here. All Jews hoped the Messiah was about to come in some vague way. For Simeon, the promise was more specific. Emanuel, God With Us, was about to be *born*, and could be expected and looked for among the firstborns being presented daily at the temple. Naturally, as days, weeks, months, and years passed, doubts arose. These joined the growing feelings of weariness that had come with age and with long-delayed gratification.

This day, however, Simeon woke with a start. There was a vigor in his body that was unfamiliar. Sitting on his bed he paused a while as he stared at the laced sunlight streaming through the lattice window. Could this be the day? He knew he could not ignore this stirring within him. As he walked up the Temple steps, he prayed under his breath, "Show me the one, Lord."

Three sets of parents suffered Simeon to peel back the swaddling that morning for a peep. Simeon, as always, smiled and entered into the joy of each couple as much as he could but no baby seemed to possess what he was looking for. And just what was he looking for? A warm glow? An ethereal light? A fuzzy feeling? All he would have said was, "I don't know, and I often worry that I have missed him, but God promised me that I will not die until I see him. So I hang on to His promise."

Suddenly, one couple, huddled around a bundle, caught his eye as they gingerly handed their bundle to a priest. Simeon approached and had a peep. Finally, he knew he had not made it all up, that he had not missed the Messiah's arrival, and that, in his heart, he really did know what he was looking for. His weary hope was now peering in at the answer. His heart began to feel like it would burst with the urge to let the whole world know who this child was. As the Spirit moved him, he declared what his heart saw: that this child was to be God's salvation, not only for Israel, but a light that would bring revelation to the nations of the earth.

Text: Luke 2:25–35

Prayer: Lord, I come to you again asking that you would give me a heart to wait patiently and confidently for your promises, and eyes to see it when it comes. Amen

9

Just What You Were Looking For

Some of the lines from films live permanently inside my head. Sometimes this is through sheer over-exposure: my girls tend to have a favorite movie that they watch over and over, and they make me watch it with them. I am not even allowed to sleep, though I am usually provided with a book to read. *Frozen* is the one that springs to mind at the moment, and *Mary Poppins* before that, both of which were an improvement on the Barbie movies of recent years. At other times, a one-liner seems to stick because of its poetic brevity. Script writers tend not to waste words so they get their characters to say very profound things, yet always with that believable colloquial feel that a line from a film ought to have. In this category I would place a brief conversation in *Forrest Gump*. It is the hippie era and everyone seems to be finding Jesus. Cynically, Lt. Dan says to Forrest: "Have you found Jesus yet?" To this Dan replies, "I didn't know I was supposed to be looking for him."

And this is the story of Anna the Prophetess: a woman who knew what she was looking for. She is estimated to have been about one hundred and five years old. She spent much time at the temple and, like Simeon, must have done so with a strong sense of expectation.

She enters the court where the holy family are and where Simeon still is as he explains in a soft voice to Mary all the sorrows that will come on her because of her Son's special calling. Anna, instantly bursts into praise. She absolutely knows who this child is, and this is what the passage says: "She spoke of him to those who looked for redemption in Jerusalem." She spoke of him to those who looked for him. She spoke of him to those who longed for release, for deliverance, for redemption.

And this takes us to the heart of what the gospel message is and how it works. In fact, in a sense, she is the first ever evangelist. What is the good news? It is simply a piece of information. It is the information that God has invaded, that heaven has invaded earth, and things are going to be different now. News of an invasion is not normally greeted with cheer. Horror and dread must have come upon the Poles when Germany invaded, dismay upon the Kuwaitis when Iraq invaded, anger upon the Iraqis when Britain and America invaded. Invasions are usually about the imposition of the will of another, and though the invasion of God is of a different quality, news of it of course, has never been what the majority of people want to hear. Most people are dismayed that God wants to interrupt their lifestyle, horrified and afraid about what he is going to do. But, the way God has invaded is entirely different from the way humans go about invading. Invading as a baby is highly unusual for a start. But more than that, we see from the teachings of the adult Jesus that God has the most enormous respect for human free will. He tells parables about how God's message is like seeds, some of which might land on inhospitable soil and never grow, and about a trader in pearls that finds a pearl that is beyond price and immediately sells everything he has to buy it. Jesus anticipates that some people will be like the hard ground and not produce a crop, and that a voluntary response in humans is part of the package, like the pearl trader reacting to what he found. The reign of this king, it seems, utterly depends on people declaring themselves on the side of the king. The one who, more than anyone, could use force if he wanted to and finally defeat evil, does not do so because the main seat of all evil lies buried in a pretty awkward place, a place he loves very much and does not wish to damage in any way: the human heart.

Another line of a film that has stuck is the moment when, in *Bruce Almighty*, Morgan Freeman, as God, says to Bruce, "You can have all my powers but you can't mess with free will." Where a human invasion is about the *imposition* of the will of another, the invasion of God aims to bring about a *fusion* of wills. Firstly, in Jesus, the divine will is joined to a human will. Jesus then becomes the bridge across which those who "look for redemption," those who are desperate for release, can walk. Their wayward wills can then be joined to the divine will and the struggle is over. One of the early church fathers put it this way: "He became such as we are so that we could become such as he is." God invades humanity; humanity is invited into God. God descends to us; we ascend to holy heights not naturally possible. The condition? Jesus simply said that we needed to humble ourselves and become like children, that we needed to believe in him. Then he gave us a reason to by rising from the dead.

Prayer: Lord I look for redemption. I look for release from the things that limit and ensnare me. I invite you to reign in me, to have your way, to do your will within my will. I have come to the realization that I cannot help myself, that you are my salvation and that only in union with you am I ever likely to see that salvation worked out. Amen

10

Signs in the Heavens

BY NOW, JESUS WAS two years old. The holy family had returned to Nazareth after performing their duties in Jerusalem. Then, for reasons not given, they move back to Bethlehem. It could be that Bethlehem had now become a very special place and they desired to go back there for a season.

It is clear they were now in a house and had forgotten the squalor of the earlier occasion. The young Jesus was happily toddling around getting his fingers into everything and had mastered enough Aramaic to make his hunger, thirst and desires known to his parents from day to day.

As I write, my son is also two years old. Quite what he would make of gold, frankincense and myrrh being brought to him at this point I'm not sure. Undoubtedly he would be more interested in the lid of the box containing the gold than the gold. He would open it, then shut it, then be unable to open it again: "Can't open it Daddy." Then, he would shut it again, and be unable to open it again and start crying. Soon, the myrrh would be all over the floor and he would make a start on the process of spreading it with his fingers. Matthew, sadly, tells us nothing of the response of the toddler Jesus to the kindly gifts pressed upon him that day.

As to the wise men, we know not whether they were three or some other number, whether they were from Arabia, Babylon,

Yemen or the Chaldees. We only know that through seemingly astrological means some men wealthy enough bring with them some valuable gifts had noticed something unusual in the sky. Again, we do not know what the star was, though there are a number of contenders, this being a period in history that can boast an unusual number of astronomical phenomena, the one most often cited being a conjunction of Saturn and Jupiter in 7BC: an event that only happens once every eight hundred years and would have produced a very strange glow in the night sky. While the majority of people then as now would have read no meaning at all into a bright star in a strange position, it signified to these astrologers something of momentous importance. And it seems that God was willing to woo them to himself by using their astrological knowledge, and, having total power over the heavenly bodies this was easy to do.

It is to Herod that the wise men go first, gaining an audience with him in his brand new Jerusalem palace. Reputedly the grandson of a Philistine temple servant and part Edomite, Herod's claim to the throne of Judah was slender indeed, so he was readily threatened by anyone with a rival claim, even a two year old lad. With reverence, the wise men ask Herod: "Where is he who is born King of the Jews?" This one question was enough to bring a cold sweat all over the fake king's puffy flesh. The Greek word used to describe his terror refers to the stirring up of water. And it seems the Jerusalem establishment was stirred up in like manner. The Roman senate had pronounced Herod "King of the Jews," back in 40BC. This title was his by right owing to his patronage of the Romans. Yet there was no erasing the paranoia he felt about the way the Jews looked upon him. He compensated for this feeling by his many great building projects, and by his murderous brutality, a quality he passed on to his grandson Herod Agrippa I, who murdered John the Baptist and was in power when Jesus was crucified.

It is a truly remarkable piece of discernment on Herod's part that, with the barest whiff of the true King of the Jews: in the form of a vague enquiry from some superstitious foreigners about a harmless infant, he knew beyond all doubt that his true rival was at large. Likewise, in the ministry of the adult Christ, it will be the demons that, with undisguised terror, recognize him first, long before any disciple calls him "Christ." And it will be the noses of the religious authorities that detect most strongly the pungent oil of the Anointed One, the smell of divine authority.

But to those who were not at war with God and were ready to surrender to him, there was only joy and delight, never the dread that filled his enemies. And this is what we have here. When the wise men find the boy, they "rejoice with exceedingly great joy." They do not feel threatened by him; they are not insecure in his presence: they spontaneously and gladly "fall down and worship him." Then they present their treasures, as was the tradition when congratulating the newly crowned. The Greek word used for joy here is closely related to the word for grace, God's unmerited favor ("chara" joy, "charis" grace). In their hearts they knew they were not worthy to see this lovely sight. They fell down beneath the weight of that feeling: so humbling yet so filled with delight, rather like discovering a beautiful photo of one of your children that you thoughtlessly took with your mobile. The moment comes when you really look and you really see that God has blessed you beyond what you could ever deserve.

Jesus then, even from the age of two, was destined to be someone that would provoke either fear or delight, dread or joy, jealousy or worship. Indifference, it seems, was not going to be a common response. Yet Christians in the West today complain that when they try to present Jesus to people, that is exactly the result. There is neither the antagonism of the brutal mobs of John Wesley's day, nor the mass repentance of the Day of Pentecost. People are respectful, but not responsive; polite but not provoked; interested even, but not changed. Makes you wonder if we've got the right Jesus.

Text: Matthew 2: 1–12

Prayer: Lord, come and be a terror to my pride and take your throne in my life. Lord come and be the joy and delight of my hungry, desperate heart. I do not deserve you but I fall down and worship you and invite you into my heart. Amen.

11

The King's Fist

"The Massacre of the Innocents" has become one of those innocuous phrases that has become the title of numerous paintings and is uttered in sophisticated circles. Renaissance artists like Rubens beautified the event with dramatic, muscular nudes, and his was followed by further similar renditions into the Baroque era, and this despite the grim realities of recent conflicts that were as fresh in people's minds as the ethnic cleansings of Rwanda and Bosnia are to ours. Perhaps religiosity had fabled and mythologized the events until they had become drained of meaning, like an over-used cliché.

And it is not my purpose here to shock us back into seeing the full horror of it but to try to capture what Matthew himself says about it. There are two words in the Greek that seem to unlock something for us: "Hina" (pronounced "Hinna") and "Tote"(pronounced Tottie). "Hina" means "so that," "in order that." It refers to something that was intended to happen. It happened on purpose and by God's design. Matthew uses the phrase to refer to the flight into Egypt: "This happened in order that (Hina) what was spoken by the prophet might be fulfilled: 'out of Egypt I called my son.'" Just after the wise men had left their endowment of wealth with Mary and Joseph and departed, an angel appeared in a dream to warn Joseph that, despite the warm fuzzy feeling this visit must have left him with, the child was not safe, and that they were all to flee to Egypt. This they did, without hesitation, under the cover of darkness.

The holy family is soon well on its way into the barren heart of the Judean Hills. Fast asleep, Jesus lies on Mary. Mary rides on the donkey. The stress having subsided, a slight sense of adventure rises within them. They had never been anywhere so exotic as Egypt before. While they are on their way, Herod has gone berserk. He already knew that the star the wise men had described had first appeared two years ago. In a fit of rage, Herod issued the decree that all Bethlehem's male children two years and younger—probably about twenty boys in all—were to be singled out for destruction in a short but horrific episode of slaughter. Here, Matthew uses: "Tote:" "Then was fulfilled what was spoken by Jeremiah the prophet: 'A voice was heard in Rama, lamentation, weeping and great mourning . . .'" He is careful not to make God the direct cause of this: it was not a "Hina," an "in order that," but a "Tote," a "then." The event could be interpreted as fulfilling something and therefore not unexpected, an event that would be woven into the overall plan. God knew that, given the temperament of Herod, when he found out that he had been outwitted by the wise men, "then" this would happen.

Primarily Matthew wants us to see in Jesus a family likeness to another great life that was also very nearly the victim of a massacre: Moses. The mention of Egypt further reinforces this mental association, as well as the prediction that Moses made: "The Lord will raise up a prophet like me from among your own people." The child was destined to be the prophet like Moses, the Messiah. And, as in the life of Moses there was a mixture of "so that"s and "then"s; of things purposed and things allowed, so with this little prophet. Both the Hinas and the Totes, as far as Matthew is concerned, add up to "fulfilled." It all fits in with the ancient biblical story.

Prayer: Lord thank you for all the times when your purposes have been fulfilled and all the blessings these brought. I do not yet fully understand the reason for the bad things you allowed but I trust that none of it takes you unawares and all of it will work for good. Amen

Text: Matthew 2:13–23

12

The Father's House

We all wish we knew more about the boyhood of Jesus. Apocryphal stories abound, mostly from the *Infancy Gospel of Thomas*. Before he even reaches the age of twelve, according to this account, he has already created sparrows from mud, struck a child dead for bumping into him, struck some people blind, and then restored them all once he'd stopped being angry (but a few years later got angry at a school teacher and struck him dead without restoring him). When his water jar broke, he gathered water miraculously into his cloak spread out upon the ground, the grain he sowed was miraculously fruitful for his father, and—get this—he was able to stretch a piece of wood until it was the same length as the other to help his father's carpentry (who obviously hadn't been following the "measure twice, cut once" rule). Finally, he miraculously healed James, the future apostle, of a snake bite by blowing on the inflamed area. Clearly, an extremely useful child to have around.

Actually, probably none of that happened. Luke's story of Jesus mostly does not fit the usual "legend" format of the period, and which the *Infancy Gospel of Thomas* tried to emulate. In Luke's Gospel, instead of miracles we have a rather fraught story about Jesus remaining behind in the Jerusalem temple during Passover, a story of a lost child.

To the curious mind, the episode raises many questions. Why did his parents not notice he was not among the Nazareth convoy until two nights had passed sleeping without him along the way? These were obviously anything but "helicopter parents." And where did Jesus sleep during this time: in the temple precincts? Perhaps most puzzling of all: why was the adolescent Jesus so surprised about the fact that his mother was completely stressed out about his disappearance? You can almost see the veins popping out of her forehead. A lesser question perhaps is, what did he eat and who fed him? Of course, we cannot expect Luke, in this condensed pericope, to be unduly interested in such details. But beyond these, and, reading between the lines now: is this whole episode not evidence of something more than growing independence? Is it not very slightly defiant? And this in a way that is not really compensated for by Luke's concluding phrase; "and he went home and was subject to them"? Perhaps this can be answered by the fact that Luke's interest in Jesus is theological, not apologetic. There is not a strong need, at this early stage of church history, to launch a strong defense, the kind of defense that Justin Martyr, in the thick of state persecution, would give his life to and for a hundred years later. Luke puts that last phrase in to assure us of the generally obedient attitude of the adolescent Jesus and leaves it at that.

There is just one phrase that Luke seems to be racing towards, and which is the climax of the whole passage. If we get waylaid by questions of detail or suspicions of rebellion in Jesus, then, as far as Luke is concerned, more fool us for missing the main point. And it is a momentous climax to the whole infancy story. It is the very first time we get to hear Jesus speak for himself. Until now, various characters have waxed extremely lyrical about the boy and a number of Hebrew prophets have been quoted to point out how the hopes and dreams of a nation are to find their fulfillment in him. Now, a story that began in the temple with the voice of an angel and Zacharias' disbelief, finishes at the temple with the voice of a wonderfully precocious twelve year old and the complete bafflement of his earthly parents.

Jesus has found himself among the rabbis who were offering question-and-answer style seminars in the temple precincts. Each teacher was surrounded by a small huddle of school age children who were moving beyond the memorization of the Torah to be introduced to the oral tradition of debating the meaning of various passages by quoting famous rabbis. Jesus has been moving from one group to another, listening intently. Whenever he opened his mouth to speak, others in the group would look round at him and stare, staggered by his luminescent grasp of the subjects being discussed.

I sometimes say to people who want to know what their special gift or calling is: "what do you do that you love so much you forget the clock." Hours and hours fly by when you are doing what you love, when you are doing you were made to do. It is like food to you. You are never wearied but always revived by doing this thing, even though it may be something that requires immense skill. To you, it is never too hard. Perhaps this is a picture of the young Jesus. Hours, even days, have passed and he has barely even noticed. He is basking and bathing and soaking in the thing which he loves: the Word and ways of God, his true Father. It may even have been a moment of discovery for Jesus: the first time he becomes fully aware of who he is. However he came by this awareness, it is already fully formed by the time he replies to his distraught parents: "How is it that you didn't know that I must be in my Father's house?"

The stage is set. The battle lines are drawn. This one simple claim: that of his special relationship to his Father and what this Father had now sent him to accomplish will now begin to bring the very best and the very worst out of people. All-forsaking allegiance and demonically-inspired hate will both appear and fight it out on the Gospel stage until finally evil seems to win, until finally, even Jesus would say, "This is your hour and the power of darkness." Then will come the great reversal, the immense victory over hell and death and evil that would put the world itself on a different trajectory and bring hope to us all.

Text: Luke 2:41–51

Prayer: Father of our Lord Jesus Christ and my Father: Like the boy Jesus lost in his Father's house, may I too come to know more fully than ever what my life's purpose is. And would you open the opportunities I need so that I too can be lost in that purpose to which you have called me. Amen.

Bibliography

Bishop, Jim. *The Day Christ was Born*. San Fransisco: Harper & Row, 1959.

Edersheim, A. *The Life and Times of Jesus the Messiah*. Grand Rapids: Eerdmans, 1971.

Farrar, F. *The Life of Christ*. London: Cassell, 1909.

Fitzmyer, J.A. *The Anchor Bible: The Gospel According to Luke*. New York: Doubleday, 1981.

France, R.T. *Matthew: An Introduction and Commentary*. Leicester: IVP, 1985.

Grubb, Norman. *Once Caught, No Escape*. London: Lutterworth Press, 1969.

Marshall, Howard, I. *Luke: A Commentary on the Greek Text*. Exeter: Paternoster, 1978.

Morris, Leon. *Luke: An Introduction and Commentary*. Leicester: IVP, 1974, 1988.

www.ingramcontent.com/pod-product-compliance
Lightning Source LLC
Chambersburg PA
CBHW060202070426
42447CB00033B/2291